GW00384245

What Christians
Should Know About...

The End-Time
Harvest

David Shibley

Sovereign World

Copyright © 1998 David Shibley

All rights reserved. No part of this publication may be reproduced,
stored in a retrieval system, or transmitted in any form or by any means,
electronic, mechanical, photocopying, recording or otherwise,
without the prior written consent of the publisher.

Unless otherwise indicated all Bible quotations are taken from
the Holy Bible, New International Version.
Copyright © 1973, 1978, 1984 by International Bible Society.
Used by permission

NKJV – New King James Version.
Copyright © 1983 by Thomas Nelson, Inc.

ISBN: 1 85240 231 8

This Sovereign World book is distributed in North America by
Renew Books, a ministry of Gospel Light, Ventura, California, USA.
For a free catalog of resources from Renew Books/Gospel Light,
please contact your Christian supplier or call 1-800-4-GOSPEL.

SOVEREIGN WORLD LIMITED
P.O. Box 777, Tonbridge, Kent TN11 0ZS, England.

Typeset and printed in the UK by Sussex Litho Ltd, Chichester, West Sussex.

What Christians Should Know About...

The End-Time Harvest

The mandate to declare God's glory to all nations has always been the commission of God's covenant people. Since the days of Abraham, the people of faith have had a clear assignment to bring blessing to all the families of the earth.

Just prior to His ascension into heaven, Jesus left His followers very clear marching orders. Once again He brought our assignment into a laser focus that we call the Great Commission: *"Go and make disciples of all nations"* (Matthew 28:19). *"Go into all the world and preach the good news to all creation"* (Mark 16:15). This commission is what the church is to be about between the time Jesus left the earth and the time He returns.

For twenty centuries the church has accomplished many noble things. Yet we have left undone the **one specific assignment** Jesus left for us. **All other pursuits** are subordinate to Christ's clear command.

Time to Refocus

I have had the honor of ministering in almost 50 nations. The beauty of the body of Christ expressed through multiple cultures is indescribable. I have drunk deeply from the refreshing wells of the church's life in many nations.

So it is more than a little disturbing to discover that Christians in my own nation are by far the most introspective believers in all the world. We often whine, "I just want to know my purpose. I've got to reach my destiny!" We race all over the country going to "Destiny Conferences" and devour tapes and books on

"Discovering Your Destiny." It would be amusing if it were not so appalling. Even cloaking our self-centeredness in Christian garb and jargon cannot cover the nakedness of this "cult of self" that is choking much of the Western church.

How can we ever hope to discover **our** purpose in the earth when we separate it from **God's** purposes in the earth? How will we ever know **our** destiny when we have so little identification with **God's** destiny for the nations?

It is certainly good to pray, "Lord, what is Your will for my life?" But it is far better to pray, "Lord, what is Your will for my **generation**? How do You want my life to fit into Your plan for my times?" Pursuing **God's** purposes, not ours, is the path to personal fulfillment.

Jesus wasn't kidding when He warned that those who would be self-protective in His kingdom are actually those most at risk. *"For whoever wants to save his life will lose it, but whoever loses his life for me and for the gospel will save it"* (Mark 8:35).

It is time for all this pathetic navel-gazing in the Western church to stop! We must refocus; off of our purpose and on to God's purpose, off of our own needs and on to the needs of others. William Booth, founder of the Salvation Army, was consumed with a passion for Jesus and a desire to lift others in His name. General Booth lived in a day of many inventions, including the telegraph. One day a wealthy philanthropist offered to telegraph one of Booth's sermons worldwide. Booth immediately accepted the offer.

"There is one stipulation," the philanthropist cautioned. "Your sermon can be only one word long." General Booth was quick to comply. Here is Booth's masterpiece: a one-word sermon:

"Others."

William Booth took seriously Paul's admonition in Philippians 2:4-11,

Each of you should look not only to your own interests, but also to the interests of others. Your attitude should be the same as that of Christ Jesus: Who, being in very nature God,

4

did not consider equality with God something to be grasped, but made himself nothing, taking the very nature of a servant, being made in human likeness. And being found in appearance as a man, he humbled himself and became obedient to death – even death on a cross! Therefore God exalted him to the highest place and gave him the name that is above every name, that at the name of Jesus every knee should bow, in heaven and on earth and under the earth, and every tongue confess that Jesus Christ is Lord, to the glory of God the Father.

The church does not need to be bogged down (or fogged in) by an identity crisis. Nor do you. Our purpose is clear. The Great Commission could not be more lucid. As Thomas Coke, founder of the world missions movement among Methodists observed, we are "embarked on the most glorious and most important work in the world."[1]

This is God's Hour for End-Time Harvest!

A biblical Greek word, *kairos,* describes a unique season of possibilities. By sovereign grace, God has chosen that your life be woven into "the *kairos* hour" for world evangelization. When Scripture uses this word, it is usually in reference to a brief, specific season of God's favor. Using this word, Jesus refers to a "time of harvest" in Matthew 13:30 (NKJV) and Paul speaks of a "due season" for reaping in Galatians 6:9 (NKJV). And in such *kairos* seasons of opportunity, the Bible urges us to be "redeeming the time" (Ephesians 5:16 NKJV). One translation reads, "Buy up the opportunities."

Our current era is a season the Bible would describe as the fullness of time. Throughout history God has made major transitions in His dealings with humanity in two thousand year increments. This leads many Christians to believe that extremely momentous events are poised to occur. As we race toward a new millennium, it is difficult to overstate the importance of the next few years for world evangelization.

For roughly two thousand years the church has been under mandate to disciple all nations. To put it bluntly, we have failed. But now, for the first time in two millennia, almost every major stream of Christianity is giving world evangelization top priority. On every continent, with the possible exception of North America, the church is advancing. And even in North America and Europe, there are hopeful signs of deep spiritual hunger.

Consider these exciting facts:

❋ During the twentieth century, Christianity has become the most extensive and universal religion in history.

❋ There are now more Christians in the Southern Hemisphere than in the Northern Hemisphere. The new centers of vitality for the church in many ways are in Africa, Asia and Latin America. This more than counterbalances the decline in the North Atlantic nations.

❋ Each day welcomes a net global increase of at least 176,000 Christians.

❋ Each week approximately one thousand new churches are planted in Asia and Africa alone.

❋ Christianity is now a genuinely international family of faith. Christianity has surged ahead in the world's less developed countries. From being predominately white, Christianity is now an amalgam of the races and peoples of the world, with whites dropping from more than 80 percent to about 35 percent.

❋ The proportion of Christians to the whole population will increase in Asia more than in any other region of the world.

Even secular analysts like John Naisbitt in his book *Megatrends 2000* predict a simultaneous series of worldwide revivals. The Chinese character for the word *crisis* well illustrates our current situation. The Chinese word is composed of a mix of the characters of two other words: **danger** and **opportunity**.

Consider the dramatic political changes that are occurring almost weekly. Some call it "crisis;" spiritually alert believers should see it as both "danger" **and** "opportunity."

Just as God demolished the formidable walls of Jericho, He is destroying walls of opposition today. This is why Dick Eastman, international president of Every Home for Christ, refers to this season as the "Jericho hour" for world harvest. "Recent miracles in once dark places globally give us cause for great hope," Eastman writes. "I truly believe this is the Jericho hour for the body of Christ. But we must capture the momentum of this season of suddenlies if our generation is to witness closure of the Great Commission."[2]

As you read, I believe the Holy Spirit is stirring you. He prods you today, much as Mordecai did when he asked his niece, Queen Esther, *"Who knows whether you have come to the kingdom for such a time as this?"* (Esther 4:14 NKJV). You have not picked up this little book by accident or chance. God is speaking to you! He has brought you to the kingdom for such a time as this!

The breakup of the old Soviet Union and the opening of the eastern bloc nations to the gospel at the beginning of the 1990s was something of a trial balloon the Holy Spirit was sending up. He was saying to us, "What will you do with mega-opportunities? Will you be a righteous steward of this *kairos* season? Will you finally seize your destiny and align your life's purpose with the purposes of God in your generation?"

Now the compelling question comes to you: So **what?**

What will **you do** in light of the hour God has placed you in history?

Do you have a sense of stewardship of these fantastic opportunities?

Will you live with some sense of appreciation of these seasonal challenges for the gospel's global advance?

Will you pray, think and strategize globally?

Will you live for eternity, realizing that at the Judgment Seat of Christ you must "give an account of your stewardship" in these momentous days?

Or, when you stand before the Lord, will you try to sputter out a reason for being spiritually comatose, "business as usual," through the most hope-filled hour of harvest in two thousand years?

As one looks at the colossal needs and even more colossal opportunities, one wants to cry out with Jeremiah, *"Is it nothing to you, all you who pass by?"* (Lamentations 1:12).

Well… is it?

Does it make any difference to you? Will anyone be in heaven who would not otherwise have been there because you faced these questions today? Will this confrontation result in transformation… in you? In nations?

If not, why don't you spare yourself the effort and stop reading now.

It is precisely this scandal of an unbroken heart that impedes evangelism today. We need a fresh baptism of the kind of compassion that led William Booth to suggest that if he could, he would include fifteen minutes in hell in the training of all Salvation Army officers. He knew that would keep their priorities right and prepare them for a life of urgent, compassionate ministry.

Are there any left today who weep instead of sleep, agonizing before God for the lost? Glorious harvest is promised to those who have sown in tears. *"Those who sow in tears will reap with songs of joy. He who goes out weeping, carrying seed to sow, will return with songs of joy, carrying sheaves with him"* (Psalm 126:5-6). The crown of rejoicing awaits those who win souls (see 1 Thessalonians 2:19-20). *"Those who are wise will shine like the brightness of the heavens, and those who lead many to righteousness, like the stars for ever and ever"* (Daniel 12:3).

Harvest Passion

In the Book of the Revelation, two sickles are thrust into the earth. The second is a sickle of global judgment. But prior to judgment, a sickle for gathering is placed into the earth to reap an international harvest of souls. That first sickle is being swung across the earth's ripe fields of spiritual harvest, even as you read this book. *"Take your sickle and reap, because the time to reap has come, for the harvest of the earth is ripe"* (Revelation 14:15).

The immensity of the crop of souls requires passionate harvesters. Even now, the Father is employing eleventh hour workers for the end-time harvest. But at this late hour He is only interested in those who will work, with no thought to the hours or energy it will require.

I recall standing on Brighton Beach and drinking in the crisp sea breeze as it washed across my face. It was summer, 1992. As I looked out toward the European continent I thought back to a very different time but the same place.

It was the same scene, Brighton Beach, but the year was 1850. Hudson Taylor, still a teenager and only recently converted, surrendered his life to God for China on this wind-swept sandy beach. In the aftermath of that experience with God at Brighton, Taylor said, "I feel that I cannot go on living unless I do something for China." Hudson Taylor sailed for China in 1853 and later founded the China Inland Mission.

The ramifications of that commitment at Brighton are still being felt in China today. In fact, Ruth Tucker asserts that "no other missionary in the nineteen centuries since the apostle Paul has had a wider vision and has carried out a more systematized plan of evangelizing a broad geographical area than Hudson Taylor."[3] Taylor, like Paul, possessed a passion for harvest.

As the salt water sprayed my face I prayed, "God, do it again."

Hudson Taylor's life priority was to bring the gospel and its social lift and blessings to the people of China. He was clearly focused on fulfilling Christ's Great Commission in the vast reaches of China's inland. As he matured in his walk with the Lord, Taylor would discover what he termed "the exchanged life," as he learned to rely on the dynamism of the indwelling Christ rather than human strength to get the job done.

As with Paul before him, once he encountered Jesus Christ, Hudson Taylor's priorities were radically and eternally changed. Along with Paul, he felt that he was a debtor to bring the gospel to those who had not heard it. And with Paul he pursued the vision with a whole-hearted passion. Paul wrote, *"I am obligated both to Greeks and non-Greeks, both to the wise and the foolish. That is why I am so eager to preach the gospel also to you who are at Rome"* (Romans 1:14,15).

But this kind of language, much less this kind of passion, is extraneous to many Christians today. To be sure, we continue to speak of **vision**, but we seldom speak of **burden**. We hear much about **destiny** but almost nothing about **dying to self**. We exult in **the joy of the Lord** but **travail for souls** is foreign to us. Such agonizing for the lost might even be viewed by some as a "lack of faith." This generation of Christians speaks of **self-fulfillment**. Taylor's generation of believers understood **self-sacrifice**. Ironically, those who practiced self-sacrifice ended up a lot more self-fulfilled and self-actualized than most Christians today!

Why? Because they embraced the veracity of the Bible's clear teaching that one truly "finds" his or her life only in laying it down for Christ and for the gospel.

Look at the shift of focus. No longer is the object God or even others. The new center of attraction is self! Have we lost a sense of accountability for the lost condition of humanity?

Any church that is not seriously involved in world evangelization has forfeited its biblical right to exist! Any Christian who just flat doesn't care whether or not people crash into eternity without God does violence to the heart of the gospel and the heart of Jesus. Such a Christian is a walking paradox, no matter how orthodox his or her theology may be.

Yet many Christians are completely unmoved by the fate of the unconverted and wholly disinterested in the purposes of God in their generation. The same Christians who yawn with boredom when *missions* is mentioned are often impassioned in their denunciations against society's sins.

Hey, don't we get it? Lost people are just acting – lost! Unsaved people are just acting – unsaved! If we **really** want to see the social order redeemed and morality restored, we'd better get back into seeing **people** redeemed and restored!

But maybe there's something far more sinister at work here. Perhaps **our** hearts need to be changed every bit as much as the hearts of the unconverted. Too many of us are just like Jonah; we don't **want** to see the unrighteous find mercy. We enjoy thundering God's pronouncements of judgment but the prospect that pimps, terrorists and rapists might actually repent and find

10

forgiveness sends us into a psychological tailspin, just as it did Jonah. In fact, Jonah was so "depressed" over God's kindness, he wanted God to take his life!

After Jonah had trumpeted his prophetic warning to debauched Nineveh the city came clean before God with heart-felt repentance. But was Jonah pleased that God's mercy had overridden His judgment? Hardly! "I knew that you are a gracious and compassionate God," Jonah whined. "I knew you would be slow to anger and abounding in love toward these perverts. I knew you would relent from sending calamity on these swine! Just what kind of God **are** you, anyway?"

Good question. Here's a small part of the answer. Unlike the Hindu gods, He is perfect and only one omnipotent God suffices for every human cry for divine intervention. Unlike the Muslim concept of Allah, God goes far beyond mercy to bestow grace and relationship to undeserving sinners. Unlike the concept that even some Christians have of God, because of the cross of Christ, God's first disposition toward humanity is love, not judgment.

And lest we forget, it's because God **is** "gracious, compassionate, slow to anger, abounding in love" that **we** ever got into His family!

Baptism of Compassion

Yet God is more than willing to give us a fresh baptism of compassion. He wants to perform "eye surgery" on us so we can bring things back into proper focus. Are you willing for such a surgery?

If you're willing, I challenge you to pray two dangerous prayers. First, **ask the Holy Spirit to pour out God's love into your heart.** The Bible says, *"God has poured out his love into our hearts by the Holy Spirit, whom he has given us"* (Romans 5:5).

Let God wash away the anger and bitterness, replacing it with His love. After all, love is the most potent weapon in the Christian's arsenal. You can counter words with words. You can counter rhetoric with rhetoric. You can counter bombs with bombs. But aggressive love – how do you counter *that?*

Second, ***ask God for the gift of tears.*** How lacking this is today. Yet the Bible says, *"Those who sow in tears will reap with songs of joy. He who goes out weeping, carrying seed to sow, will return with songs of joy, carrying sheaves with him"* (Psalm 126:5,6).

God has given us precious seed, the seed of the gospel. May He grace us to water that seed with tears. I am not suggesting that we become emotional basket cases. But perhaps the truly emotionally imbalanced are not the sensitive but the **insensitive**. Some Christians seem to see tears as incompatible with victorious, faith-filled living. Yet those who weep are in good company because *"Jesus wept"* (John 11:35).

When conditions warrant it we ought to weep. Daily I pray that I will not go through these last minutes of the twentieth century in some kind of spiritual stupor, drugged by entertainment or indifference and thus unresponsive to humanity's agonies.

The Day of Visitation

Do you remember the dramatic scene when Jesus stood outside the city of Jerusalem and wept over its impending destruction? Jesus was literally moved to tears *"because you did not know the time of your visitation"* (Luke 19:44 NKJV).

This is God's hour of visitation for global spiritual harvest. God has sovereignly ordained that this generation of believers have within its grasp what earlier generations of Christians could only dream of – closure on the Great Commission. We must be honorable stewards of this precious gift of a global visitation of God's Spirit for harvest.

I live and work every day on three premises. First, because I am a part of the renewal of God's Spirit in the church, I bear a heightened responsibility to evangelize the world. I espouse the present-day working of the Holy Spirit, complete with the possibility for all of the manifestations of His gifts. Since I endorse miracles and faith up front, this heightens my responsibility to be a world Christian.

Second, because I am a part of the church in the affluent Western world, I bear a heightened responsibility for world evangelization. While the power of the global church has shifted to the church in less developed nations, the Western church still bears heightened responsibility for world harvest because of our affluence and influence. Most of the Bible schools and Christian publishing houses are in the Western world. Churches with the largest budgets are in the Western world.[4] This only augments our global accountability.

Third, because more people are receptive to the gospel than ever in history, this too augments our responsibility to give world evangelization top priority. **The Holy Spirit has orchestrated the events of this planet to indicate that world evangelization must be our top priority for the remainder of this century and until the Lord returns.**

Mordecai reminded his niece, Queen Esther, that she had been brought to the kingdom "for such a time as this." God had sovereignly intersected Esther's life with a one-chance, go-for-broke, win-it-all-or-lose-it-all situation. Just so, God has sovereignly orchestrated events to mesh a worldwide renewal with a once in a lifetime opportunity. By sovereign grace, it has fallen on our generation to have within our grasp that for which other generations of Christians could only dream – closure on world evangelization.

If not us, who? If not now, when? If it is not this generation of Christians – we who have seen God's gracious renewal, we who possess more data on global harvest than any previous generation, we who stand on the shoulders of twenty centuries of missionary giants – if it is not us God wants to use to evangelize the world, then **who else** is it?

And if we are not to throw all our hearts and energies into the global harvest now – as the Spirit sweeps from nation to nation, now that we have actually isolated the remaining 1739 unreached peoples, now as eschatological hopes are escalated as we face a new millennium – then, **when** will there be a more opportune time?

I am not suggesting that we run off in all directions, merely with human energy that is fueled by a noble cause. I **am** urging that we be imbued with the spirit of the sons of Issachar *"who understood the times and knew what Israel should do"* (1 Chronicles 12:32). May we too have an understanding of our times to lead God's people in what they should do. This is no time to be idle, it's a time to work long hours by the Spirit's empowering in the Father's ripe vineyard. As we work, let's remember that harvest is seasonal. Urgency should press us on. Jesus said, *"As long as it is day, we must do the work of Him who sent me. Night is coming, when no one can work"* (John 9:4).

Global Impact Praying

John Wesley often remarked, "The Holy Spirit, in answer to prayer, does everything." He also cautioned, "You can do more than pray *after* you have prayed but you can do nothing but pray *until* you have prayed." Prayer is the highest call of all.

This is hard for many Western Christians to learn since we tend to be activists. But since we also tend to be pragmatists, we should be praying far more than we are. Why? Because in a word, prayer works!

Some 50 million Christians targeted the 1,739 people groups that still have no Christian witness in the massive Praying Through the Window III effort in October, 1997. Hundreds of thousands pray systematically for nations using Patrick Johnstone's *Operation World* (a goldmine of missions data), and thousands more use the excellent daily *Prayer Journal* published by Youth With A Mission. The Church Prayer Network coordinates churches to pray in cooperation with Joshua Project 2000. The Prayer Track of the AD 2000 & Beyond movement also coordinates international prayer efforts. And the World Prayer Center and Jericho Center in Colorado Springs are activating non-stop intercession until closure to the Great Commission is a reality! If Christians today are uninformed regarding prayer for nations and unreached peoples it's not because of a lack of information!

It's especially encouraging to note that since the Praying Through the Window efforts began in the early part of this decade, the number coming to Christ every day worldwide has jumped by some 100,000 people! Dr. David Barrett suggests that as many as 170 million Christians worldwide are committed to praying daily for awakening and world evangelization, and there may be as many as twenty million believers who see intercession as their primary calling.[5]

It is these unknown multitudes, not necessarily the high-profile Christians, who are well-known in the heavenlies. They are "closet world-changers," because from their prayer closets they are impacting the flow of history. Paul Billheimer reminds us:

> "The praying people are the body politic of the world, and the church holds the balance of power in world affairs. Not only in the future ages is she the ruling and governing force in the social order, but even now, in this present throbbing moment, by means of her prayer power and to the extent to which she uses it, the praying church is actually deciding the course of human events. Some day we shall discover that prayer is the most important factor in shaping the course of human history."[6]

Indeed, Billheimer would go on to say, "the fate of the world is in the hands of nameless saints."[7] Suppose that Dr. Billheimer is only half right. Should that not still be sufficient motivation to move us to intercede for peoples and nations? *Prayer is the vehicle whereby the hearts of peoples and nations are prepared to receive God's offer of salvation.*

Dick Eastman adds his voice of experience in the world prayer movement to challenge us to prayer. Eastman writes,

> "I am becoming increasingly convinced that the emerging global call to pray will be the key to gathering in history's final and greatest harvest. To bring back the King, we must pray back the King."[8]

One day Christ will dominate the whole universe. David Bryant reminds us that "revival is God's way of shepherding history toward great climax."[9] An eminent theologian of colonial

America, Jonathan Edwards, said,

> "A universal dominion is pledged to Christ, and in the interim before the final consummation, the Father implements this pledge in part by successive outpourings of the Spirit…"[10]

So, come Holy Spirit! Renew Your deeds in our day, in our time make them known! Empower us for our great assignment! Oh, Lord, may Your kingdom come, may Your will be done *on earth* as it is in heaven!

And now this call to pray comes to you. Prayer is the one mission to the world that all Christians can share. As always, God is searching for "gap people." One of the saddest verses in the Bible is Ezekiel 22:30, *"I looked for a man among them who would build up the wall and stand before me in the gap on behalf of the land so I would not have to destroy it, but I found none."*

❉ Will **you** stand in the gap for the nations?

❉ Will **you** become a "house of prayer for all nations"?

It was a season of prayer initiated by young people – what is now referred to in history as the Haystack Prayer Meeting – that launched the world missions endeavor in America. Another prayer effort of young people throughout the Global Consultation on World Evangelization in Seoul, Korea signaled that God is raising up a new generation of young intercessors for our day. As concerts of prayer rise to the throne from believers in every nation, we will see Satan's fortress toppled and the kingdom of God established.

Dr. C. Peter Wagner often says with rejoicing that "the international prayer movement is out of control!" Thank God, it's true! It is simply too big to quantify. And yet – and yet, there remains a desperate need for new recruits into the international prayer army. I'm calling on you today to become, in Dick Eastman's words, a "harvest warrior" who wars for the harvest through your praying and giving.

Further, the last few years have seen a weaving together of intercession, spiritual warfare and worship as mighty tools to break open nations and peoples for the gospel. Literally hundreds of prayer walks throughout the 10/40 Window have helped loosen the grip of long-standing demonic strongholds. Skilled intercessors and prayer warriors are carefully but confidently engaging major powers of darkness in strategic level spiritual warfare. Never has there been such an assault in the heavenlies on the evil principalities and powers. Prophetic declarations of worship over yet unreached peoples are boldly proclaiming the inevitable rule of Jesus Christ over *every* tribe, people and nation. We should praise God that we have lived to see the emergence of this great global prayer movement.

Get involved today in global impact praying! Starting today, your prayers can make a world of difference. It is the great condition of the Great Commission.

Early Church Missions Strategy

This is a decade rife with supernatural phenomena. In the Western world, our sterile technology has created a thirst for metaphysical experience. Many try to satiate this thirst by flirting with Eastern religions, psychic networks or the occult. Yet this thirst can never be truly satisfied until we come to the One who said, *"If anyone is thirsty, let him come to me and drink"* (John 7:37). Heaven-initiated experiences of supernatural power are the powerful, effective antidote to the proliferation of unclean, other-worldly phenomena.

As Jesus said in Acts 1:8, the fullness of the Holy Spirit is given for the purpose of effective Christian witness. The great expositor D. Martyn Lloyd-Jones saw a direct correlation between the anointing of the Holy Spirit and evangelism.

> "Go through Acts and in every instance when we are told either that the Spirit came upon these men or that they were filled with the Spirit, you will find that it was in order to bear a witness and a testimony."[11]

17

Now, as in the church's inception, the great missions need is not greater harvest but more laborers. I do not believe that God's desire is merely to empower select individuals to experience the miraculous. He longs to empower His whole church! *"You shall receive power when the Holy Spirit comes on you."* The power of the Holy Spirit verifies the gospel and enables us to be Christ's witnesses to the ends of the earth. Notice that it wasn't gifted healing evangelists who were the first wave of missionary advance; it was the everyday followers of Jesus, just like you and me. *"Then the disciples went out and preached everywhere, and the Lord worked with them and confirmed his word by the signs that accompanied it"* (Mark 16:20).

Paul reveals his missions strategy for bringing the nations under the sway of the gospel when he writes that he brought the Gentiles to faith by word, deed and signs and wonders (see Romans 15:18-20). This holistic ministry of gospel proclamation, compassionate deeds and the working of miracles was tremendously effective at the beginning of the church era. It works equally well in our time.

Our only hope of seizing this *kairos* moment in missions is to partner with all world Christians and link arms in the power of God's Spirit to gather the glorious harvest.

What the Spirit is Saying to the Churches

If there is one irrefutable message God is speaking to the body of Christ today it is **reconciliation**. We are to be reconciled across denominational, racial, gender and national barriers, demonstrating the true spiritual unity for which Jesus so passionately prayed in John 17.

Having been reconciled with our brothers and sisters, we are then to take up the call to be ministers of reconciliation. **Reconciliation is at the heart of the missions mandate.**[12]

Jesus forcefully attacked the ethnic pride and provincialism of His own disciples by forcing them to travel through Samaria and interact with the Samaritans. Jesus' ministry to the woman at the well is a clear indication of how He Himself lovingly reached

18

across ethnic and gender barriers to meet the needs of this precious, victimized woman. Later in ministry to the Samaritan village Jesus showed tremendous compassion and quickly accepted the Samaritans' invitation to stay in their village for a few days (much to the disciples' chagrin, no doubt).

Jesus was kicking the provincialism out of His disciples then and He continues to kick the provincialism out of His disciples today. If you are going to be a disciple of Jesus and follow Him, you follow where He leads, and where He is leading is into uncomfortable territory to interact with those whom you may not even like and with whom you share no common heritage.

As ambassadors of Jesus Christ we are called upon to be ministers of reconciliation. Certainly, at its very core, we are to be proclaimers of the gospel that reconciles people to God. But we also are to exhibit a lifestyle of reconciliation.

God is calling us to a **reconciliation**. Also, He is calling the church to **restructure**. There is a clear call today to cell-based churches. Throughout the 1980s, effective cell-based churches were found almost exclusively in Asia. But today churches whose primary meeting points are in homes and offices are flourishing on every continent. In the eighties, cell groups in American churches were almost exclusively "nurture groups" for Christians. But today many American churches are experiencing great success in evangelism through cells. In Latin America the "Principle of Twelve" is providing explosive growth for many churches. I do not know all the reasons why the Holy Spirit is so forcefully endorsing this method of church growth worldwide. Perhaps it is because every member receives better spiritual care and there is greater accountability in smaller groups. Perhaps God is preparing the church worldwide for more intense persecution and cells are something of a warm-up for a renewed "catacomb" ministry. Maybe it's simply because it's a biblical pattern to teach *"publicly and from house to house"* (Acts 20:20). Whatever the reason, let's hear what the Spirit is saying in this area.

Finally, God is **restoring** all His gifts to His church. In the last few years there has been a major emergence in the apostolic and prophetic offices of ministry. The Bible says that the church is literally *"built on the foundation of the apostles and prophets,* *with Christ Jesus himself as the chief cornerstone"* (Ephesians 2:20). I believe these two offices are now providing what has until recently been two glaring missing keys in world evangelization. Apostles provide great impetus for massive church growth movements. Prophets can deliver *rhema* words to nations and national leaders that can provide favor and an entrance for the gospel.[13]

Friends, Family and Partners

As the church's center of gravity continues to shift from Western nations to Latin America, Asia and Africa, there is much give and take and many fabulous lessons we are learning from one another. I've had the privilege of worshiping with the body of Christ on every continent. Hues of color, diversity and emphasis only underscore to me the beauty of Christ's bride, His church.

"His intent was that now, through the church, the manifold wisdom of God should be made known to the rulers and authorities in the heavenly realms" (Ephesians 3:10). In the original language, the *manifold wisdom of God* literally translates as the *multi-colored wisdom of God!* The unique expression of each culture in its redeemed form, mixed with the beauty of every other culture redeemed by Christ's blood, creates the richest mosaic possible. In other words, God puts the multi-cultural church on triumphal display to demon powers!

Across many different nations and cultures, we are brothers and sisters through faith in Christ. Now we must proactively become friends with one another, honoring the strengths that come from the church in every nation. Fellowship is based upon our theological foundation of having the same Father. We have been born of the same Spirit and purchased by the same precious blood of our Lord Jesus. The Western church learns humility and faith from the church of the Two-Thirds World. The church of the Two-Thirds World learns vision and structure from the Western church. Who benefits? The kingdom of God benefits!

Friendship in missions has a long and glorious history, punctuated with various epochs of selfish ambition. However, even back in the days of the apostle Paul, Paul commends the Philippian church as being *"loyal yoke-fellows"* who have *"labored side by side"* with him in the gospel. The Philippians had entered into partnership with Paul on his missionary endeavors by sending him material support. By doing so, they have also entered into his suffering as Paul himself has experienced the fellowship of the suffering of Christ.

With a few notable exceptions in the Western world, Christians today are experiencing one of three phases of attack: harassment, persecution or martyrdom. It is clear that we are to rejoice with those who rejoice and weep with those who weep. As we identify with the body of Christ, holding hands as friends and then as partners in advancing the gospel to the yet unreached peoples of our world, we see God's hand of grace and share both the sufferings and the triumphs of the church around the world.

Missions' Terminal Generation

The role of the Western church in missions is changing dramatically. That is why God called me at the beginning of the 1990s to stop conducting my own evangelistic crusades to other nations. Rather, He instructed me to "lift up the hands" of national pastors, evangelists and church leaders in order to enable them to fulfill their God-given dreams and visions for the harvest. Since that time, Global Advance has provided training and tools for over 100,000 native pastors and church leaders in over 30 nations. God has given us a vision to train one million leaders to plant one million new churches worldwide. Our new role is to affirm, undergird, encourage and partner with indigenous churches and their leadership around the world.

Changes in the makeup of global evangelicalism have been astounding. The message from God's Spirit to all of us is clear. We need one another. The Western church needs the Two-Thirds World church. The Two-Thirds World church needs the Western church. They need our fellowship, not just our money. We need their wisdom, not just their anointing.

It has been estimated that there are some nine million Christian churches worldwide. It has also been suggested by several missions analysts that at least another nine million churches are needed to bring closure on the Great Commission. If this three-fold cord of churches, mainline denominations, traditional evangelicals and Pentecostals and charismatics continues to entwine, together we can see "a church for every people" within the next few years.

God is also weaving a strong cord of at least three generations of missions leadership: older, younger, and the young. The great, post-war leadership of the church is fast departing from the scene. The recent deaths of several pioneers signal a passing of the torch to men and women in my age bracket who represent the younger leadership. We are not the post World War II era of leadership. Many of us are products of the Jesus Movement of the late sixties and early seventies. God is raising up a powerful cadre in my own nation of mission leaders among this younger group. However, we too are in our mid-40s and beyond. Now the Holy Spirit has His eye on the young. I believe those sometimes referred to as *Generation X* are poised to make the greatest contribution to missions of any generation in Christian history. God has raised up ministries like Teen Mania and Youth With a Mission to help produce a generation of missions leadership for a life-sized challenge.

God has specifically spoken to me to invest my life in this young generation of emerging missions leadership. That is why I've committed a large amount of time in 1999 to a world tour of Bible colleges. I want to pour my heart and passion into emerging church leaders around the world. And I want to hear their hearts as well. I want to lay hands on them and I want them to lay hands on me. The Holy Spirit is calling us to link generations of missions leadership for the greatest global harvest ever.

Today's youth are also sometimes referred to as *the Terminal Generation*. While some may feel this is a stigma of doom, I believe it is a prophetic declaration going back to the very root Latin word *terminus*, meaning fulfillment or completion of a season of time. One hundred years ago the missionary statesman John R. Mott prophesied, "The worldwide proclamation of the gospel awaits accomplishment by a generation which shall have the obedience, courage and determination to attempt the task."[14] With all my heart I'm convinced that God will give today's Christian young people the grand prize for which twenty centuries of believers have prayed, worked and dreamed – closure on the Great Commission!

We are currently in a once-in-a-lifetime opportunity regarding world evangelization. Nevertheless, I would not want you to think that I am merely championing a cause, even a cause as noble as the evangelization of the world. What I am urging upon all of us is that we so freshly fall in love with Jesus Christ that what is precious to Him becomes precious to us and what is priority for Him becomes priority for us. Jesus is very clear about what that is. He said, *"The Son of Man has come to seek and to save that which was lost"* (Luke 19:10 NKJV).

You are a chosen generation. God has allowed your life to intersect with one of the most exciting times in all history. You have the privilege of helping set the time-table of heaven's eschatology. In times like these, God's word calls us to both holiness and evangelism. **It is time for every Christian and every church to be awakened to their full and thrilling potential.**

The new missions leadership that drafted the Declaration at the Global Consultation on World Evangelization understands this. Hear well these stirring words from the Declaration:

> "We confess a deep awareness of our failure in the past to do all we could have done to make Christ known throughout the world, especially in the areas where no church movement exists. We also repent of our needless divisions and competitive attitudes that have hindered the advance of the Gospel. We resolve, by God's grace, to no longer ignore the challenges, nor miss the opportunities set before us. This is the time for which we were born."

God did not make a mistake when He sovereignly ordained that you bear Christ's name and embrace His cause as we enter a new millennium. For reasons known only to our omniscient God, He didn't want Wesley, Spurgeon or Moody for this hour of witness.

He wants **you!**

Finding Where You Fit

I am often rebuffed when I challenge Christians in this way with the statement, "Well, not every Christian is called to be a missionary." I tend to agree. Not everyone of us has giftings in cross-cultural ministry. But **every Christian** is called to be a witness for Jesus Christ and **every Christian** is called to missions. There is a difference between being called to be **a missionary** and being called to missions. Not every believer has the missionary gift, but every Christian is called to some kind of involvement in missions. We are all called to advance the gospel in some way and to participate in the fulfilling of God's purposes in our generation.

There is a role God wants you to play in helping to fulfill His purposes in this hour. It is a role tailor-made for you and only you can fill that role. How do you find where you fit in missions?

Your most important step in seizing today's great missions opportunities is to *prayerfully examine your role in today's harvest.* Every Christian should be either a **go-er**, a **pray-er**, a **giver**, an **encourager** or an **advocate**. There are at least three of these roles that every believer should embrace. We should all be **pray-ers, givers** and **encouragers.**

Does God want you to be a **go-er** – part of the great international missionary force? God is still calling out **career** missionaries to devote major portions of their lives to cross-cultural, hands-on missionary service. Perhaps He wants you to give a significant slice of your future to Him as a **short term** missionary. Or perhaps you should just start by being part of a **team** missions outreach from your church or a credible missions organization.

You can play a significant role in global harvest this very day by being a **pray-er**. There are excellent resources available to help you pray intelligently and systematically for every nation and unreached people group. Also, pray for missionaires and national pastoral leaders you may know by name. Don't forget to pray over current events, asking the Holy Spirit to engineer the circumstances in every nation to draw people to Christ.

I challenge you to begin now to be a **giver**. Above the tithe to your local church you should give specifically for the advance of the gospel both at home and worldwide. Give to your church's missions outreaches, to missionary families and to worthy missions ministries. Many Christians are now earmarking at least one percent of their income directly for frontier missions to unreached peoples.

Above all, be an **encourager**. Look for opportunities to give a word of encouragement to missionaries, indigenous pastoral leaders and all those involved in spreading the gospel. Just think what one phone call or note could mean to weary soldiers of the cross on the frontlines.

Finally, consider becoming a missions **advocate**. Offer to serve on your church's missions committee. Offer to help in missions conferences. Become the most knowledgeable person you can be on the subject of world evangelization. And when it comes time for your influence to make a difference, be an advocate for the world's physically and spiritually poor. Don't miss any chance to make an impact for Jesus because the dark side of the history of missions is the tragedy of missed opportunities.

I am tired of hearing about "closed doors" to the gospel. I agree with what Brother Andrew has said: "There are no closed doors to the gospel – provided that, once you get inside, you don't care if you ever come out."

And even if doors are closing, new windows of opportunity are opening all the time. The church must be poised to crawl rapidly through these seasonal open doors. If ever there was a time to rise to the challenge and in the Spirit's power attempt great things for God, that time is now. This can be the church's finest hour.

More than anything I have mentioned, however, is the need for a complete devotion to Jesus Christ. A commitment to the cause of Christ flows naturally out of a commitment of love to Him.

Shortly before David Livingstone died, he was offered a final opportunity to come back to the accolades that were certainly due him. He was asked, "Why, Dr. Livingstone, are you living in obscurity when your name is a household word in the 'civilized' world? Why are you living here in poverty when your books are best sellers, both in Britain and the United States? Why are you fighting these tropical diseases when we have new medical treatments you could avail yourself of in Britain?" Livingstone replied that he had long ago made a promise both to God and to the Africans he so dearly loved that he would live and die in Africa. In fact, after his death in a posture of prayer in an African hut, before his body was returned to England for burial in highest honor at Westminster Abbey, as per his instructions, his heart was cut out and forever buried in African soil.

Livingstone wrote these words in his diary shortly before his death: "My Jesus, my King, my life, my all – I again dedicate the entirety of my life unto Thee."

What will it take to finish the job and plant a church for every people group and get the gospel to every person in our lifetime? A new generation must arise who will say from their hearts, "My Jesus, my King, my life, my all – I again dedicate the entirety of my life to You."

For God Alone

Certainly we should honor the faithful obedience of every missionary effort, both past and present. At the same time, we need to refocus much of our thinking about world evangelization. The Holy Spirit wants to shift our focus from merely **local** thinking to **global** thinking; from a **temporal** orientation to an **eternal** orientation. Most of all, He wants to turn us from **man-centered** missions to **God-centered** missions.

Much of the missions enterprise has been centered around people – the physical and spiritual plight of humanity and the obligation of Christians to respond. In our missions preaching we have appealed to duty, we have cajoled with guilt, we have prodded with inspiration. I know, I've done it myself. But again, where is God?

For the last several years I have blushed with embarrassment as I've watched too many fellow Christians massage **their** egos, luxuriate in **their** creature comforts and infer that the ultimate purpose of God is **their** happiness and well-being. I rejoice in the genuine moves of God's Spirit in recent years. But even when God brings revival – are revivals just for **us?** Where are all of our "feel good" revivals taking us?

Are we as insensitive as the nine lepers who went their merry way once they were healed? I have no problem with thousands of Christians "doing some serious carpet time." But I have a major problem with those who stay light-headed once they get up from the carpet and continue living without a clue as to **His** honor, **His** glory and their role in fulfilling **His** purposes in the earth! The purpose of revival is to empower the church to fulfill her global mission!

While embracing signs and wonders, it is time to mix **power evangelism** with **glory evangelism**. In any given situation among the nations, God may or may not demonstrate certain types of His powerful acts. But He **always** desires to reveal His glory. He wants to be honored through the uniqueness of every culture He Himself has created. It was this longing for God's glory to be manifested among all peoples that drove early Christians into missions. *"It was for the sake of the Name that they went out..."* (3 John 7).

People are eternally lost without Jesus Christ. Surely that should make us missions activists, but it is not our highest motivation. The needs of humanity are immense and desperate. Yes, we should identify with their suffering and seek to heal the open festering wounds of our world. Yet, though noble, this is not to be our highest motivation. Talk of "discovering our destiny" may be the right motivation or it may be just more thinly veiled narcissism. If "fulfilling our purpose" just means finally figuring out what our gifts are and getting a kick out of using them, we're carnal narcissists, no matter how much we may protest to the contrary. But if "fulfilling our purpose" means throwing all of our energies, gifts and influence into extending His glory throughout the earth, then we're getting the point!

With Paul, our highest motivation should be to offer all peoples to God as trophies of His grace that He might receive the worth and honor that is due only to Him. He lived to see *"the Gentiles* [the nations] *...become an offering acceptable to God, sanctified* *by the Holy Spirit"* (Romans 15:16). It's no wonder that the new song of the redeemed from every tribe, language and people peals out with the loud declaration, *"Worthy is the Lamb, who was slain, to receive power and wealth and wisdom and strength and honor and glory and praise!"* (Revelation 5:12).

In this once in a lifetime bumper crop harvest, we need to focus on God's glory among every people, not just the size of the harvest. *Our service and love is not first to the harvest, it is to the* **Lord of the harvest**! We crave His honor in all the earth. Charles Wesley expressed it magnificently in his paean of praise, *O For a Thousand Tongues:*

> *My gracious Master and my God*
> *Assist me to proclaim,*
> *To spread through all the earth abroad*
> *The honors of Thy Name!*

God's Honor and Our Integrity

What is the greatest detriment to the evangelization of the world today? You may be surprised at my answer. I lay the blame for our failure not at the feet of Muslims, belligerent governments or disinterested secularists. **The greatest impediment to world evangelization today is the carnality of the church!**

Someone has well remarked that the church has survived through many centuries both the wrath of its enemies and the ineptitude of its members. Nevertheless, the ineptitude of those who name the name of Christ is by far a greater problem than the wrath of our enemies. In fact, Christianity seems to thrive in the soil of persecution. The fastest growing church in the world today is in China, yet the Chinese government has harassed, persecuted, imprisoned, and sometimes martyred Christians since communism came to power in the early 1950s. When Western missionaries were forced out of China, there were one million Christians. Today there may be as many as one hundred million believers in China, making it the nation in the world with the most Christians.

Jesus said, *"You are the salt of the earth... you are the light of the world"* (Matthew 5:13,14). As such, He commands us to *"...let your light shine before men, that they may see your good deeds and praise your Father in heaven"* (Matthew 5:16).

Everywhere we look people and nations are in desperate need. We are called to be salt and light, but Jesus warns that we are not to lose our saltiness nor are we to allow our light to grow dim. Sin short-circuits God's purpose in our lives, destroying our saltiness and dimming our light. The things that wreck people's lives are just multiple variations on a few sordid themes: the abuse of money, the abuse of sex, the abuse of power, the abuse of alcohol and drugs, poor time management, and the adopting of an embittered attitude. As believers who are focused on God's purposes in our generation, we are to renounce every deadening influence of sin.

In light of the impending Day of the Lord, Peter asks the piercing question, *"What kind of people ought you to be? You ought to live holy and godly lives as you look forward to the day of God and speed its coming"* (2 Peter 3:11-12). In the days in which we live, we are *"to live holy and godly lives."* This is only possible as we draw upon the resources of the Holy Spirit.

So how does this all shake down in modern life? It means that we as world Christians are not only focused on getting the gospel to the ends of the earth and establishing viable churches among all unreached peoples; it also means that we are allowing the Holy Spirit to daily transform us into the very image of Christ. We welcome the cultivation of His fruit and the release of His gifts. In very practical ways it means that:

1. World Christians are **faithful people**. We are faithful to our vows. We are faithful to our spouses. We are faithful to God. We are faithful to our churches. We are faithful to our employers. We are faithful to show up at work. We are faithful to give an honest day's work. We are faithful to pay all our bills on time. We are faithful to serve humanity in the name of Christ, serving in His name and as a gift to Him.

2. World Christians are **people of integrity**. There is no duplicity

in our lives. We are who we say we are. The public persona and the private person are one and the same. Although we are not perfect, we hold up the ideal of the person of Jesus Christ and believe God's word when He commands us, *"Be holy, because I am holy."* (1 Peter 1:16).

3. World Christians are **accountable people**. We get in small groups of accountability and allow the hard questions to be asked of us. I am deeply grateful for my friendship with Mike Downey, president of Global Missions Fellowship. We meet together as executives of two mission organizations to hold each other accountable in our personal lives. Each time we meet we ask each other the following questions.

Since we last met...

> – *Have you had a daily time with the Lord?*
> – *Have you been completely above reproach in all your financial dealings?*
> – *Have you fulfilled the mandate of your calling?*
> – *Have you been with a woman in a way that could be perceived as inappropriate?*
> – *Have you sought out any explicit or pornographic material?*
> – *How is your marriage?*
> – *Have you just lied?*

4. World Christians are **expectant people**. Peter said we are to live godly lives as we look for and actually speed the return of the Lord (2 Peter 3:11,12). We are to expect the return of Jesus Christ. We also, in some amazing way, actually hasten His return. God allows us the high dignity of participating in His very timetable by helping to fulfill the Great Commission. Jesus said, *"And this gospel of the kingdom will be preached in the whole world as a testimony to all nations, and then the end will come"* (Matthew 24:14). That means that we can actually hasten heaven's eschatology by seeing "a church for every people and the gospel for every person."

John Wesley transformed two nations by his call to holiness.

He well understood the imperfections of his own life, but he stated, "I will preach holiness until I am holy. I will preach sanctification until I am sanctified." We are not authorized to dilute the message or God's call to a holy life simply because we fall short of it.

In July of 1983 I was honored to attend the International Conference for Itinerant Evangelists in Amsterdam. From that meeting a biblical standard for evangelists emerged. It became something of a code of standards for Christian evangelists worldwide. Affirmation VIII declares,

> "We acknowledge our obligation, as servants of God, to lead lives of holiness and moral purity, knowing that we exemplify Christ to the church and to the world."

Commenting on this affirmation, Billy Graham wrote,

> "Preaching is not the only way we declare the gospel of Christ. Our lives also should be witnesses to others of the reality of Christ. Those who have affected me most profoundly in my life have not necessarily been great or eloquent preachers, but men and women of God whose lives were marked by holiness and Christ-likeness. The gospel must be communicated not only by our lips but by our lives. This is a visual proof that the message we preach actually can change lives.
>
> "Our world today is looking for men and women with integrity, for communicators who back up their ministry with their lives. Our preaching emerges out of what we are. We are called to be a holy people – separated from the moral evils of the world.[15]

For the flames of revival to spread, for the purposes of God to be enacted, we must be salt and light. When the great American evangelist of the last century, J. Wilbur Chapman, was in London, he had an opportunity to meet General William Booth, who at that time was past eighty years of age. Dr. Chapman listened reverently as the old General spoke of the trials, the conflicts and victories.

> The American evangelist then asked the General if he would disclose his secret for success. "He hesitated for a second," Dr. Chapman said, "and I saw the tears come into his eyes and steal down his cheeks, and then he said, 'I will tell you the secret. God has had all there was of me. There have been men with greater brains than I, men with greater opportunities; but from the day I got the poor of London on my heart, and a vision of what Jesus Christ could do with the poor of London, I made up my mind that God would have all of William Booth there was. And if there is anything of power in the Salvation Army today, it is because God has had all the adoration of my heart, all the power of my will, and all the influence of my life.'"[16]

Will you, by the power of the Holy Spirit, raise a standard of integrity so that the world may know there is a God who transforms lives? Will you allow the light of Jesus to permeate through your personality so that men and women will be pointed to Him? God only knows the impact that could occur when you lay before Him all the adoration of your heart, all the power of your will, and all the influence of your life.

Even after suffering numerous injustices for the name of Jesus, Paul said, *"Christ's love compels us"* (2 Corinthians 5:14). That is what keeps us going, even when all other sources go dry. Even faith is fueled by love (see Galatians 5:6). How then is love itself fortified? The Bible says that *"God has poured out his love into our hearts by the Holy Spirit, whom he has given us"* (Romans 5:5). As noted missionary Elisabeth Elliot has said, "The love of Christ constrains us. There is no other motivation for missionary service that is going to survive the blows of even the first year. You do it for **Him**."[17]

A passion for Jesus and His global and eternal purposes must consume us. I'm convinced there comes a point in every Christian's life when he or she makes some crucial life choices. Either you fall victim to the spirit of the age and embrace the cult of self or you live on a higher plane. The godly Francis Xavier challenged the apathetic European students of his day to "give up their small ambitions and come and preach the gospel of Christ."

So, what about you? Which will it be? Are you going to live to please yourself or to bring international acclaim to His name? Nobody's twisting your arm. The choice is entirely yours. But, remember this: **What you choose really does matter, both for your future and the future of our world, and you will give an account for your choice.**

We must not allow the overt persecution of antagonists, the well-intentioned tugs away from the harvest fields by Christians or the apathy of the carnal to deter us. Whether we battle "fightings from without" or "fears from within" we must stay committed to Christ and His purposes in our generation.

Far too many Christians are "couch-potatoing" their way through life, either ignorant of or indifferent to God's glory in the earth and His purposes for our time. Suddenly they realize that the sand has sifted through the hourglass. They're out of time, out of touch, and, if they do go to heaven, they will go there out of treasure. They will have accomplished the sum total of nothing of eternal value.

I'm calling you today to a higher life. And I'm asking God to use this book to jolt thousands out of apathy and allow them to seize our once in a lifetime opportunity.

In the late 1940s an American newspaper reporter was stationed in the city of Shanghai, China. He watched from the balcony of his hotel one horrific night as Mao Zedong and troops loyal to Mao pillaged the city and burned much of it to the ground. The reporter watched as much as his stomach would allow. Finally he walked back into his room, sat at a little desk and wrote these words,

Tonight Shanghai is burning, and I am dying too.
But there's no death so real as the death inside of you.
Some men die by shrapnel and some go down in flames,
But most men die inch by inch, playing little games.

Whatever else you may do, don't die inch by inch, playing little games. Live for what matters. And what matters is the exaltation of the Son of God to the ends of the earth.

1. Cyril Davey, *Mad About Mission* (Basingstoke, Hants: Marshall Pickering, 1985), 115.

2. Dick Eastman, *The Jericho Hour* (Lake Mary, Fla.: Creation House, 1994), 21.

3. Ruth A. Tucker, *From Jerusalem to Irian Jaya* (Grand Rapids: Zondervan, 1983), 173.

4. The financial power structure of the global church is rapidly changing. New centers of financial strength for the twenty-first century church will probably be in Asia, notably in places like South Korea, Singapore and perhaps as communism wanes, Hong Kong.

5. David Barrett and Todd M. Johnson, *Our Globe and How to Reach It: Seeing the World Evangelized by A.D. 2000 and Beyond* (Birmingham, Ala.: New Hope, 1990), 27.

6. Paul E. Billheimer, *The Technique of Spiritual Warfare* (Santa Ana, Cal.: TBN Press, 1982), 58.

7. Paul E. Billheimer, *Destined for the Throne* (Fort Washington, Penn.: Christian Literature Crusade, 1975), 106.

8. Dick Eastman, *The Jericho Hour* (Lake Mary, Fla.: Creation House, 1994), 25.

9. David Bryant, *The Hope at Hand* (Grand Rapids: Baker, 1995), 48.

10. Ibid., 48.

11. D. Martyn Lloyd-Jones, *Joy Unspeakable* (Eastbourne, England: Kingsway, 1984), 75.

12. I encourage you to read John Dawson's excellent book in this series for more on this vital topic.

13. See David Cannistraci, *The Gift of the Apostle* (Ventura, Calif: Regal, 1996).

14. David Shibley, *A Force in the Earth* (Lake Mary, Fla.: Creation House, 1997), 85.

15. Billy Graham, *A Biblical Standard for Evangelists* (Minneapolis, Minn., Worldwide Publications, 1983), 73.

16. Paul Lee Tan, *Encyclopedia of 7700 Illustrations* (Rockville, Md.: Assurance Books, 1977), 1367.

17. David Shibley, ed., *Challenging Quotes for World Changers* (Green Forest, Ark.: New Leaf Press, 1995).

If you have enjoyed this book and would like to help us to send a copy of it and many other titles to needy pastors in the **Third World**, please write for further information or send your gift to:

Sovereign World Trust, P.O. Box 777, Tonbridge, Kent TN11 0ZS, United Kingdom

or to the **'Sovereign World'** distributor in your country.